Weeds

POETRY, PROSE, WIT AND WISDOM

KENEBEC MEDIA

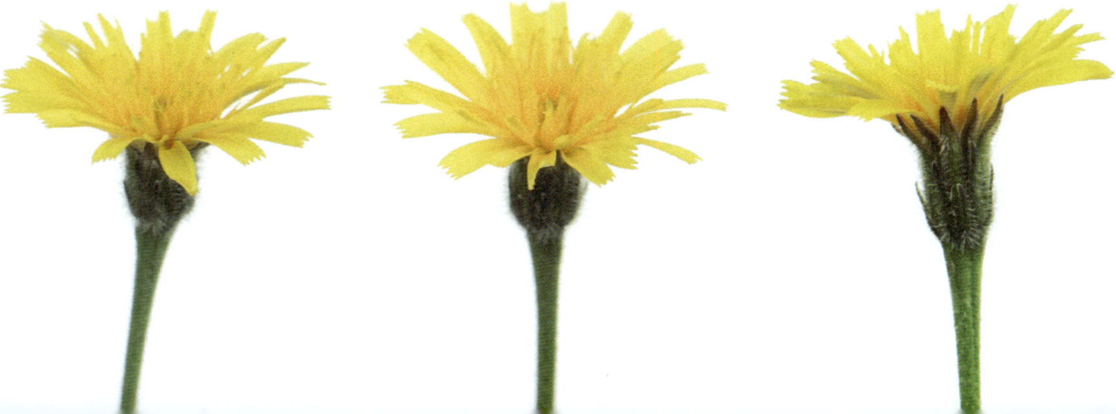

Weeds

POETRY, PROSE, WIT AND WISDOM

COMPILED AND ILLUSTRATED BY
VAL AND GREG DUNCAN

MANY THINGS grow in the garden
that were never sown there

THOMAS FULLER, 1654-1734
GNOMOLOGIA

THE DIFFERENCE
between a flower
and a weed
is a judgement

ANON

I HAVE PRETTY MUCH come to the conclusion, that you have got to put your foot down in gardening. If I had actually taken counsel of my friends, I should not have had a thing growing in my garden to-day but weeds. And besides, while you are waiting, Nature does not wait. Her mind is made up. She knows just what she will raise. The most humiliating thing to me about a garden is the lesson it teaches of the inferiority of man. Nature is prompt, decided, inexhaustible. She thrusts up her plants with a vigour and freedom that I admire; and the more worthless the plant, the more rapid and splendid its growth. She is at it early and late, and all night; never tiring, nor showing the least sign of exhaustion.

CHARLES DUDLEY WARNER, 1829-1900
MY SUMMER IN A GARDEN

CUT A THISTLE in May, it will be back the next day
Cut a thistle in June, it will be back soon
Cut a thistle in July, it will surely die

OLD SAYING

A WEED is but an unloved flower

ELLA WHEELER WILCOX, 1850-1919

I CAREFULLY SOWED a rare seed
And I gave it all it would need
It grew very fast
But when it flowered at last
It turned out that my plant was a weed!

LIMERICKS AND TRIMERICKS FOR GARDENERS

THE GARDNER had not need be an idle or lazy Lubber, for so your Orchard, being a matter of such moment, will not prosper, there will ever be something to do. Weeds are alwaies growing, the great Mother of living Creatures, the Earth, is full of Seed in her Bowels, and any stirring gives them the heat of the Sunne, and being laid near day, they grow.

WILLIAM LAWSON, 1553-1635
A NEW ORCHARD AND GARDEN

I SCARCELY DARE TRUST MYSELF to speak of the weeds. They grow as if the devil was in them. I know a lady, a member of the church, and a very good sort of woman, considering the subject condition of that class, who says that the weeds work on her to such an extent, that, in going through her garden, she has the greatest difficulty in keeping the ten commandments in anything like an unfractured condition. I asked her which one? but she said, all of them: one felt like breaking the whole lot.

CHARLES DUDLEY WARNER, 1829-1900
MY SUMMER IN A GARDEN

I ALWAYS THINK OF MY SINS when I weed. They grow apace in the same way, and are harder still to get rid of.

HELENA RUTHERFORD ELY, 1881-1920
A WOMAN'S HARDY GARDEN

ONE year's seed
SEVEN year's weed

OLD SAYING

SMALL HERBS have grace
GREAT WEEDS do grow apace

WILLIAM SHAKESPEARE, 1564-1616
RICHARD III

THE BORDERS TOO I'd clean with nicest care
And not one smothering weed should harbour there:
In trifling thus I should such pleasure know
As nothing but such trifles could bestow.

JOHN CLARE, 1793-1864
FROM THE WISH

WHAT WOULD BECOME OF THE GARDEN if the gardener treated all the weeds and slugs and trespassers as he would like to be treated?

T H HUXLEY, 1825-1895

PERHAPS IF WE COULD PENETRATE Nature's secrets we should find that what we call weeds are more essential to the well-being of the world, than the most precious fruit or grain.

NATHANIEL HAWTHORNE, 1804-1864
OUR OLD HOME

WHAT IS A WEED?

A plant whose virtues have not yet been discovered

RALPH WALDO EMERSON, 1803-1882
FORTUNE OF THE REPUBLIC

GIVE A WEED AN INCH
and it will take a yard
And the neighbour's yard
as well !

GREG DUNCAN

A REALLY LONG DAY OF WEEDING is a restful experience, and quite changes the current of thought. For some people it is more efficient than a rest cure. It is pleasantest to take a nine-hour day of such work when the earth is wet, or even in rain, because weeds come up more easily, root and branch, from wet earth. I never want an hour at noon for dinner, like the hired man, but would prefer to lunch like horses from a nosebag. It would save time, and especially the necessity of cleaning oneself. After such a day my fingers are bleeding, knees tottering, back bent, dress muddy and soaking and shoes an offence to my tidy maid; but I have attained the most profound inward peace, and the blessed belief of having uprooted all my enemies.

ANNA LEA MERRITT, 1844-1930

WE SOW with all the art we know
And not a plant appears
A single seed from any weed
A thousand children rears

ANON

A DANDELION is such a beautiful
flower that if it was a rare plant
we would all long to grow it

ANON

A CHARMING STORY about dandelions was once told by Mrs Clive. She had been showing a visitor around her beautiful gardens. This lady was not a gardener herself, but was anxious to complement her hostess. Not knowing the names of any of the lovely flowers growing in the garden, all the lady could think of to say was, "You do grow wonderful dandelions".

WHEN I BOUGHT MY HOUSE
I bought the garden too
But the weeds thought it was theirs
And a battle did ensue

I did not want a war
I'm a pacifist you know
But since talking did not work
I now kill them with my hoe

GREG DUNCAN

I SYMPATHISE WITH WEEDS perhaps more than the crop they choke, they express so much vigour. They are the truer crop which the earth more willingly bears.

HENRY DAVID THOREAU, 1817-1862

I HAVE OFTEN BEEN TOLD that a weed is just a plant in the wrong place, but nobody warned me that it was one that had absolutely no intention of moving out.

JENNY JONES

AS WITH THE HEART, so with the garden. If any spot, however small, is left untilled, up springs an evil weed, or it becomes a wilderness . . .

THE COTTAGE GARDENER MAGAZINE, 1849

ON NO OTHER GROUND
Can I sow my seed
Without tearing up
Some stinking weed

WILLIAM BLAKE, 1757-1827

ONE IS TEMPTED TO SAY that the most human plants, after all, are the weeds.

JOHN BURROUGHS, 1837-1921
PEPACTON

. . . SO IT BEHOVES the man who would prepare the site for a pleasure garden, first to clear it well from the roots of the weeds, which can scarcely be done unless the roots are first dug out and the site levelled, and the whole well flooded with boiling water so that the remaining roots and seeds cannot germinate.

ALBERTUS MAGNUS, 13TH CENTURY

A WEED IS NO MORE THAN a flower in disguise
Which is seen through at once if love give a man eyes

JAMES RUSSELL LOWELL, 1819-1891

YET HOW AESTHETIC IS NATURE! Every spot that
is entirely uncultivated and wild, however small it
may be, if only the hand of man remains absent,
it clothes itself with plants, flowers and shrubs,
whose unforced nature and natural grace bear
witness that they have not grown up under
the rod of the great egoist, but that Nature
has here moved freely.

ARTHUR SCHOPENHAUER, 1788-1860

THE EARTH LAUGHS at him
who calls a place his own

ANON

IF I'D WANTED a low maintenance garden, I'd have planted weeds

ANON

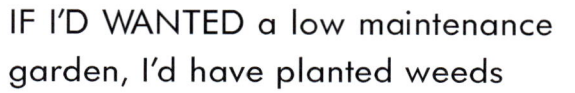

SHOULD I weed the lawn
. . . or say it's a garden ?

ANON

I AM NOT A LOVER OF LAWNS. Rather
I would see daisies in their thousands, ground
ivy, hawkweed, and even hated plantain with
tall stems, and dandelions with splendid flowers
and fairy down, than the too-well-tended lawn.

W H HUDSON, 1841-1922
THE BOOK OF A NATURALIST

ALL THESE PLANTS want constant watching, pruning,
manuring, chalking, mulching. One ought always to be
on the watch to see if things do not look well, and why
they do not. The great thing to remember is, that if a
plant is worth growing at all it is worth growing healthily.
A Daisy or a Dandelion, fine, healthy, and robust, as
they hold up their heads in the spring sunshine, give
more pleasure and are better worth looking at than the
finest flower one knows that looks starved, drooping and
perishing at flowering-time.

MRS C W EARLE, 1836-1925
POT-POURRI FROM A SURREY GARDEN

IT MUST BE ADMITTED that one of the great drawbacks to gardening and weeding is the state into which the hands and fingers get. Unfortunately, one's hands belong not only to oneself, but to the family, who do not scruple to tell the gardening amateur that her appearance is 'revolting'. Constant washing and always keeping them smooth and soft by a never failing use of vaseline — or, still better, a mixture of glycerine and starch, kept ready on the washstand to use after washing and before drying the hands — are the best remedies I know. Old dog-skin or old kid gloves are better for weeding than the so-called gardening gloves, and for many purposes the wash-leather housemaid's glove, sold at any village shop, is invaluable.

MRS C W EARLE, 1836-1925
POT-POURRI FROM A SURREY GARDEN

A FLOWER is an educated weed

LUTHER BURBANK, 1849-1926

WEEDS ARE the little vices that beset plant life, and to be got rid of the best way we know how

FARMERS ALMANAC, 1881

BUT, JUBILATE, I have got my garden all hoed the first time! I feel as if I had put down the rebellion. Only there are guerillas left here and there, about the borders and in corners, unsubdued. . . The first hoeing is a gigantic task: it is your first trial of strength with the never-sleeping forces of nature. . . The only drawback to my rejoicing over the finishing of the first hoeing is that the garden now wants hoeing the second time. I suppose if my garden were planted in a perfect circle and I started round it with a hoe, I should never see an opportunity to rest. The fact is, that gardening is the old fable of perpetual labour . . . I had pictured myself sitting at eve, with my family, in the shade of twilight, contemplating a garden hoed. Alas! it is a dream not to be realised in this world.

CHARLES DUDLEY WARNER, 1829-1900
MY SUMMER IN A GARDEN

A BOUQUET of roses looks so grand
An exotic bloom impresses
But a bunch of weeds in a child's hand
A special love expresses

VAL DUNCAN

THERE WAS an old gardener from Leeds
Who used lots of unusual feeds
Although all his flowers died
He continued with pride
To display his collection of weeds

LIMERICKS AND TRIMERICKS FOR GARDENERS

IT IS NOT ENOUGH for a gardener to love his flowers and his vegetables . . .

. . . HE MUST also hate weeds

ANON

NEVER PERFORM ANY OPERATION without gloves on your hands that you can do with gloves on; even weeding is far more effectually and expeditiously performed by gloves . . . Thus, no gardener need have hands like bears' paws.

J C LOUDON, 1783-1843
THE VILLA GARDENER

YOU CAN DRIVE OUT nature with a fork
But she will always swiftly return

HORACE, 65BC-8AD

IT TAKES ME LONGER TO WEED than most people, because I will do it so thoroughly. It is such a pleasure and satisfaction to clear the beautiful brown earth, smooth and soft, from these rough growths, leaving the beautiful green Poppies and Larkspurs and Pinks and Asters, and the rest, in undisturbed possession!

CELIA THAXTER, 1835-1894

I LEFT MY OWN GARDEN YESTERDAY, and went over to where Polly was getting the weeds out of one of her flower-beds. She was working away at the bed with a little hoe . . . I am compelled to say that this was rather helpless hoeing. It was patient, conscientious, even pathetic hoeing; but it was neither effective nor finished. When completed, the bed looked somewhat as if a hen had scratched it: there was that touching unevenness about it. I think no one could look at it and not be affected. To be sure, Polly smoothed it off with a rake, and asked me if it wasn't nice; and I said it was. It was not a favourable time for me to explain the difference between puttering hoeing, and the broad, free sweep of the instrument, which kills the weeds, spares the plants, and loosens the soil without leaving it in holes and hills. But, after all, as life is constituted, I think more of Polly's honest and anxious care of her plants than of the most finished garden in the world.

CHARLES DUDLEY WARNER, 1829-1900
MY SUMMER IN A GARDEN

HERE REMEMBER, that you never take in hand or begin weeding of your beds before the earth be made soft, through the store of rain, falling a day or two before.

THOMAS HYLL, 1528-1577

THE OUTSKIRTS OF THE GARDEN in which Tess found herself had been left uncultivated for some years, and was now damp and rank with juicy grass which sent up mists of pollen at a touch; and with tall blooming weeds emitting offensive smells — weeds whose red and yellow and purple hues formed a polychrome as dazzling as that of cultivated flowers. She went stealthily as a cat through this profusion of growth, gathering cuckoo-spittle on her skirts, cracking snails that were underfoot, staining her hands with thistle-milk and slug-slime, and rubbing off upon her naked arms sticky blights which, though snow-white on the apple-tree trunks, made madder stains on her skin . . .

THOMAS HARDY, 1840-1928
TESS OF THE D'URBERVILLES

THE FROST hurts
not weeds

THOMAS FULLER, 1654-1734
GNOMOLOGIA

YE FIELD FLOWERS! the gardens eclipse you, 'tis true:
Yet, wildlings of nature! I dote upon you,
For ye waft me to summers of old,
When the earth teemed around me with fairy delight,
And when daisies and buttercups gladdened my sight
Like treasure of silver and gold

THOMAS CAMPBELL, 1774-1844
FIELD FLOWERS

NOTHING IS AS BEAUTIFUL as spring —
When weeds in wheels,
Shoot long and lovely and lush

GERARD MANLEY HOPKINS, 1844-1889

A GOOD GARDENER MUST KNOW his weeds
as well as he knows his flowers

JENNY JONES

A GOOD GARDEN may have some weeds

ANON

DIE WHEN I MAY, I want it said of me by those who know me best, that I always plucked a thistle and planted a flower where I thought a flower would grow

ABRAHAM LINCOLN, 1809-1865

MISTRESS MARY WORKED in her garden until it was time to go to her midday dinner. In fact, she was rather late in remembering, and when she put on her coat and hat, and picked up her skipping-rope, she could not believe that she had been working two or three hours. She had been actually happy all the time; and dozens and dozens of the tiny, pale-green points were to be seen in cleared places, looking twice as cheerful as they had looked before when the grass and weeds had been smothering them.

FRANCES HODGSON BURNETT, 1849-1924
THE SECRET GARDEN

WEEDING IS A DELIGHTFUL OCCUPATION, especially after summer rain, when the roots come up clear and clean. One gets to know how many and various are the ways of weeds — as many almost as the moods of human creatures.

GERTRUDE JEKYLL, 1843-1932
WOOD AND GARDEN

THE MAN WHO UNDERTAKES a garden is relentlessly pursued . . . Hardly is the garden planted, when he must begin to hoe it. The weeds have sprung up all over it in a night. They shine and wave in redundant life. The docks have almost gone to seed; and their roots go deeper than conscience.

CHARLES DUDLEY WARNER, 1829-1900
MY SUMMER IN A GARDEN

MY GARDEN CLAIMS a good part of my spare time in the middle of the day, when I am not engaged at home or taking a walk; there is always something to interest me in the very sight of the weeds and the litter, for then I think how much improved the place will be when they are removed.

THOMAS ARNOLD, 1795-1842
LETTER TO J T COLERIDGE, 1819

IT IS SAID THAT in the eighteenth century it was believed that God had commanded that weeds should grow as a punishment for the sins of Adam. It was therefore not considered appropriate to clear the garden of weeds completely, as this would be seen as an act of rebellion against God's will.

GARDENING LORE

DAILY THE BEANS SAW ME come to their rescue armed with a hoe, and thin the ranks of their enemies, filling up the trenches with weed dead. Many a lusty crest-waving Hector, that towered a whole foot above his crowded comrades, fell before my weapon and rolled in the dust.

HENRY DAVID THOREAU, 1817-1862

A WEED IS just
a plant that is
in the wrong place

ANON

IF A WEED IS just
a plant that is
in the wrong place,
where is the right place?

GREG DUNCAN

THE CLOSING SCENES are not necessarily funereal. A garden should be got ready for winter as well as for summer. When one goes into winter-quarters, he wants everything neat and trim . . . I confess that after such an exhausting campaign, I felt a great temptation to retire, and call it a drawn engagement, But better counsels prevailed. I determined that the weeds should not sleep on the field of battle. I routed them out, and levelled their works. I am master of the situation.

CHARLES DUDLEY WARNER, 1829-1900
MY SUMMER IN A GARDEN

WHAT WEEDS I couldn't remove I buried, so that every thing would look all right

CHARLES DUDLEY WARNER, 1829-1900
MY SUMMER IN A GARDEN

NOTHING IS SO INTERESTING as weeding. I went crazy over the outdoor work, and had at last to confine myself to the house, or literature might have gone by the board.

ROBERT LOUIS STEVENSON, 1850-1894
LETTER TO SIR SIDNEY COLVIN FROM SAMOA, 1890

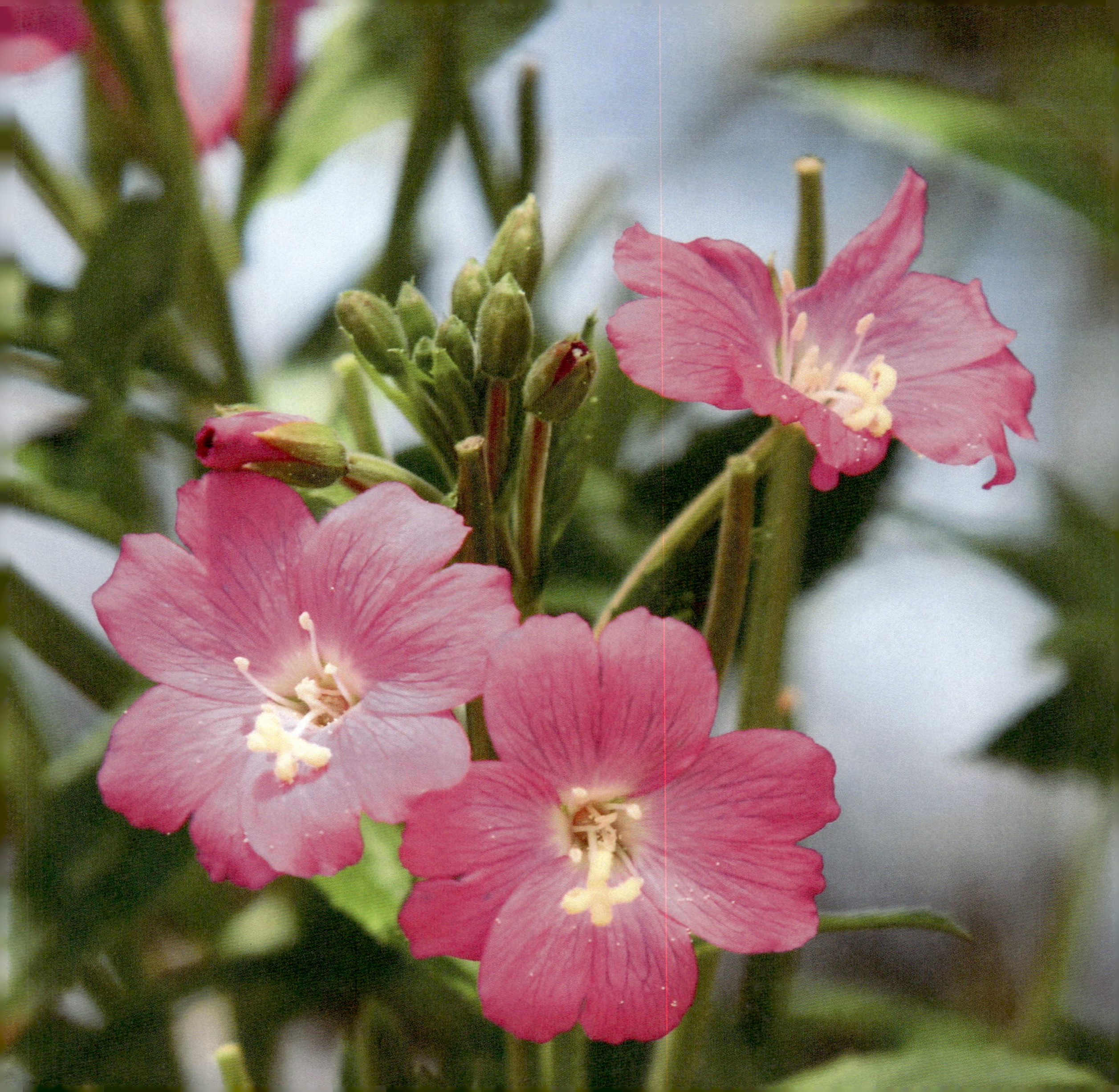

HE WHO HUNTS FOR FLOWERS will find flowers, he who loves weeds will find weeds

HENRY WARD BEECHER, 1813-1887

EVER SINCE I COULD REMEMBER anything, flowers have been like dear friends to me, comforters, inspirers, powers to uplift and to cheer. A lonely child, living on the lighthouse island ten miles away from the mainland, every blade of grass that sprang out of the ground, every humblest weed, was precious in my sight, and I began a little garden when not more than five years old.

CELIA THAXTER, 1835-1894
AN ISLAND GARDEN

A WEED IS a free-spirited flower

ANON

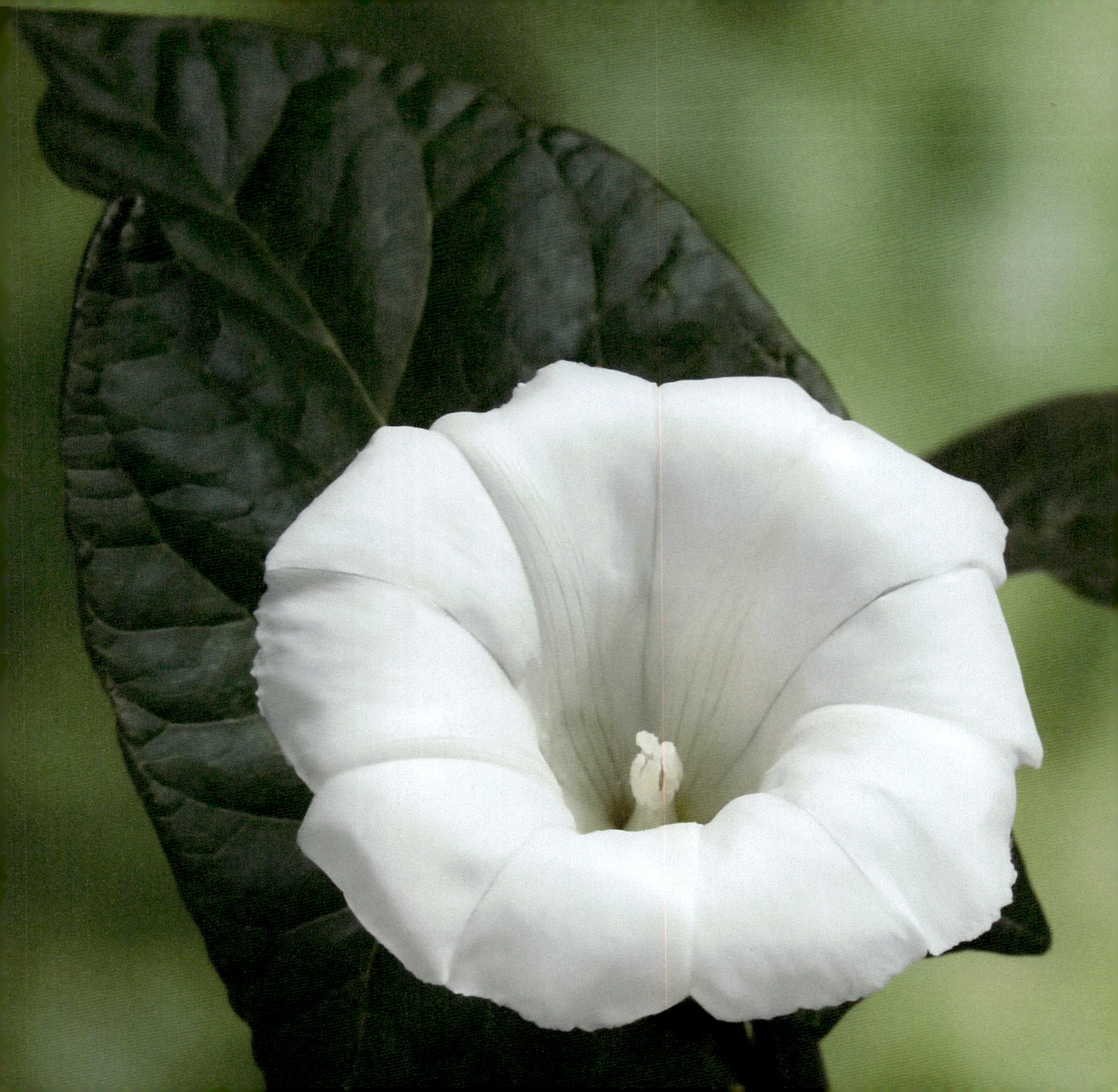

RABBIT SAT BACK IN HIS CHAIR and took a puff at his pipe. "You say you're growing weeds?"

"Yes," chirped back Mouse. "I was growing flowers but the weeds were doing better and had some lovely blooms so I decided to take out all the flowers and now I'm making a great garden just of weeds."

"Mmmm." Rabbit took another puff at his pipe. "You know you can't do that." he said.

Mouse responded indignantly. "Why not? I am and it looks beautiful."

"You may think you are, but since a weed by definition is an unwanted plant, it is logically impossible to cultivate weeds. Your weeds are now flowers and your flowers have become weeds."

Mouse furrowed his eyebrows, crinkled his whiskers and tried hard to think, but summer was not a good time for logic or thinking. So with barely a goodbye, he scurried off back to his garden to water his weeds — or as Rabbit had put it — his flowers which had been weeds until he liked them.

And then he looked at the lovely white blossom on the bindwe... bind . . . bind . . . bindflower?

It was all far too confusing for a little mouse.

GREG DUNCAN
MUSINGS OF A PHILOSOPHICAL RABBIT

I FIND THAT I keep asking why
If I neglect my flowers they will die
But as for my weeds
Ignoring their needs
Means they thrive and soon multiply

Are flowers inherently weak?
Is fragility part of the mystique?
Has selective breeding
And artificial feeding
Impaired their natural physique?

If you compare a flower and a weed
You'll see the weed's a much stronger breed
If you think I am wrong
And weeds are not strong
Just wait till they all run to seed!

LIMERICKS AND TRIMERICKS FOR GARDENERS

HE THAT HATH a good
harvest may be content
with some thistles

PROVERB

WEEDS never die

PROVERB

IN EACH HAND I hold a seed
One's a flower, and one a weed
Who should judge which one to sow?
Which has the greater right to grow?

VAL DUNCAN

IF YOU HOE when there aren't
any weeds, you won't get any

TRADITIONAL SAYING

WHENEVER I USE a garden spray
My flowers all wither
And the weeds all stay
So now the garden spray is banned
And my flowers all bloom
For I weed by hand

GREG DUNCAN

SOMEBODY HAS SENT ME a new sort of hoe . . . I do not mind saying that it has changed my view of the desirableness and value of human life. It has in fact, made life a holiday to me. It is made on the principle that man is an upright, sensible, reasonable being, and not a grovelling wretch. It does away with the necessity of the hinge in the back. The handle is seven and a half feet long. There are two narrow blades, sharp on both edges, which come together at an obtuse angle in front; and as you walk along with this hoe before you, pushing and pulling with a gentle motion, the weeds fall at every thrust and withdrawal, and the slaughter is immediate and widespread. When I got this hoe, I was troubled with sleepless mornings, pains in the back, kleptomania with regard to new weeders; when I went into my garden, I was always sure to see something. In this disordered state of mind and body, I got this hoe. The morning after a day of using it, I slept perfectly and late. I regained my respect for the eighth commandment. After two doses of the hoe in the garden, the weeds entirely disappeared. Trying it a third morning, I was obliged to throw it over the fence in order to save from destruction the green things that ought to grow in the garden.

CHARLES DUDLEY WARNER, 1829-1900
MY SUMMER IN A GARDEN

GREENFINGER

WHEN WEEDING YOU HAVE TO BE ROUGH
As you pull and you yank at the stuff
For weeds in disguise
Reach up to the skies
'Cause for weeds, The World's Not Enough

I went into my garden today
To apply a herbicide spray
But the wind was too strong
And the direction was wrong
So the weeds lived — to Die Another Day

Though it requires an element of skill
Thorough weeding can be a great thrill
You can vent your frustrations
Without complications
For with weeds you've A License to Kill

LIMERICKS AND TRIMERICKS FOR GARDENERS

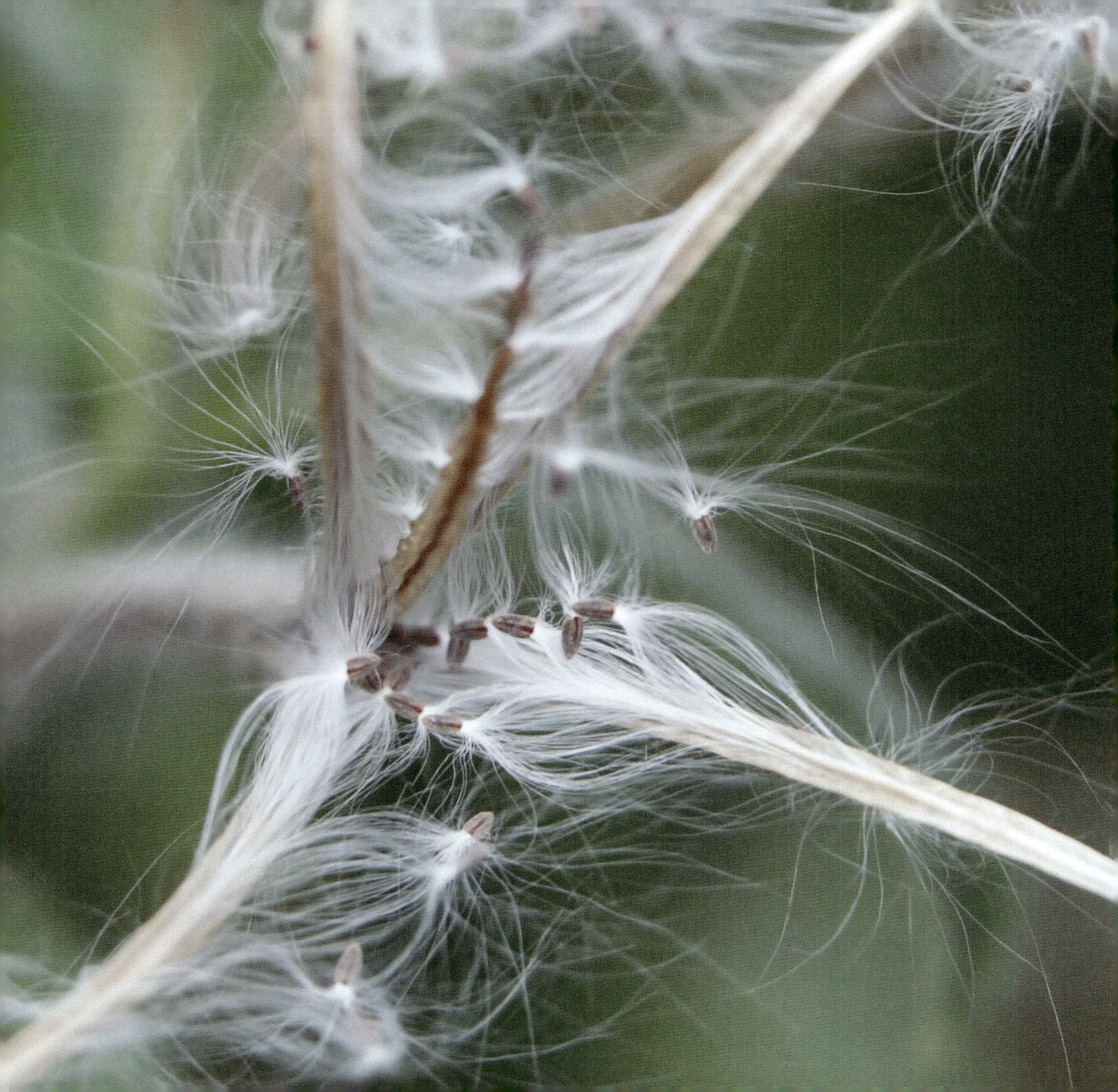

NOW 'TIS THE SPRING and weeds are shallow-rooted;
Suffer them now, and they'll o'ergrow the garden
And choke the herbs for want of husbandry

WILLIAM SHAKESPEARE, 1564-1616
HENRY VI PART II

... I WILL GO root away
The noisome weeds, which without profit suck
The soil's fertility from wholesome flowers

WILLIAM SHAKESPEARE, 1564-1616
RICHARD II

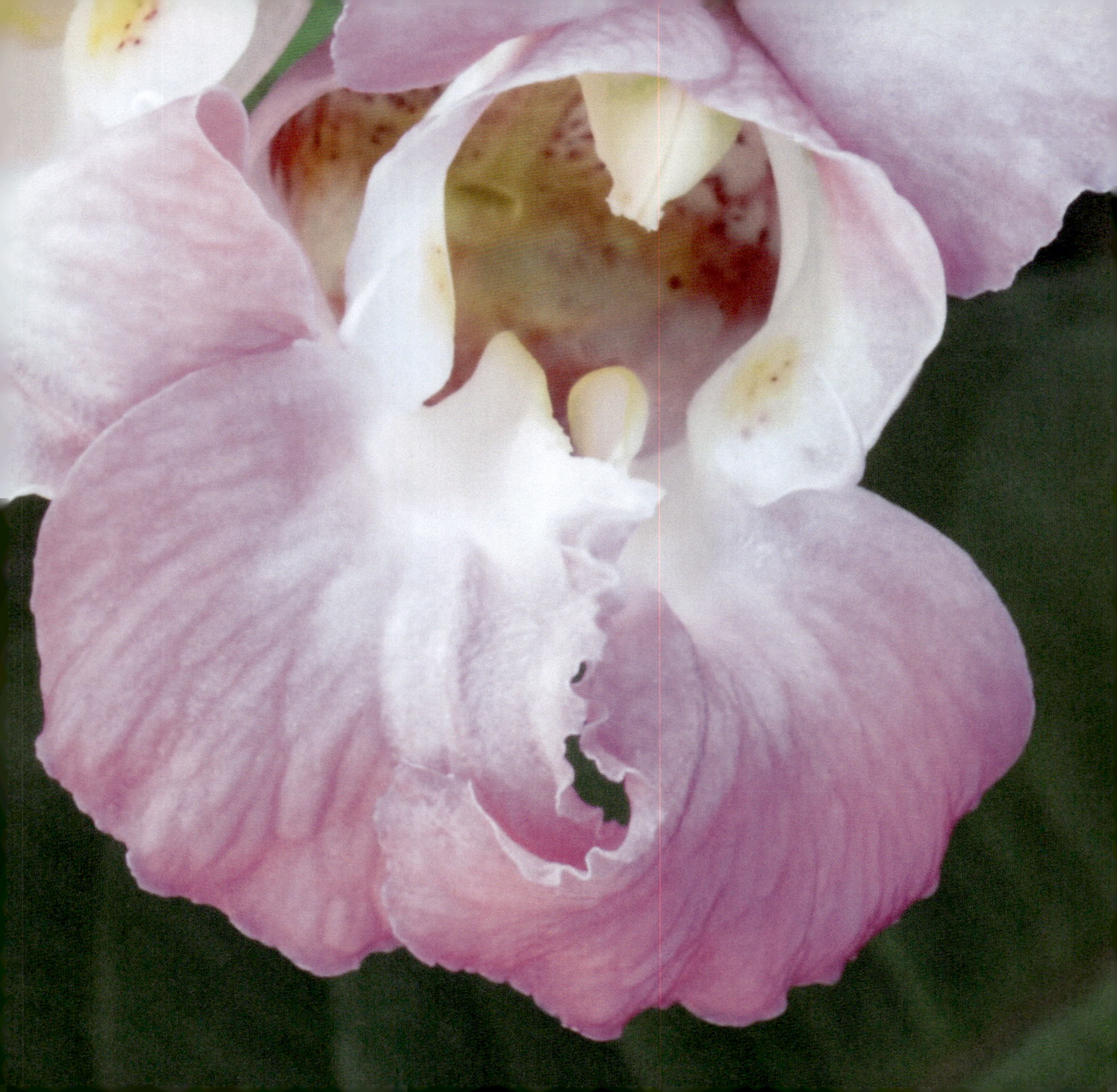

ANOTHER TERRIBLE WEED is the wild annual Balsam, *Impatiens glandulifera*, which sows itself in the most audacious and triumphant manner, but it takes little root-hold, and is easy to pull up in the spring. What a wonderfully handsome, yet delicate, plant it is! with its beautiful flowers, its long pointed leaves, its red square stems, its seed-vessels shaped like buds, which burst with a crack and scatter the seeds far and wide. Were the plant difficult to grow, no garden or greenhouse would be without it. It deserves a place, even if reduced to one plant, in every moderate-sized garden; it looks especially well grown as a single plant in good soil. To add to its perfections it has a delicate, sweet smell, and does well in water. Gardeners will always look upon it, with a show of reason, as a horrid weed; but flower-lovers will never be without it.

MRS C W EARLE, 1836-1925
POT-POURRI FROM A SURREY GARDEN

THE MUTE BIRD sitting on the stone,
The dank moss dripping from the wall,
The garden walk with weeds o'ergrown
I love them — How I love them all!

EMILY BRONTE, 1818-1848

I WOULD DEVOTE a certain part of even the smallest garden to Nature's own wild self, and the loveliness of weed-life.

JOHN D SEDDING, 1838-1891
GARDEN-CRAFT OLD AND NEW

WHAT WOULD THE WORLD BE, once bereft
Of wet and of wildness? Let them be left,
O let them be left, wildness and wet:
Long live the weeds and the wilderness yet.

GERARD MANLEY HOPKINS, 1844-1889
FROM INVERSNAID

AT WHAT POINT does a wild flower become a weed?

JENNY JONES

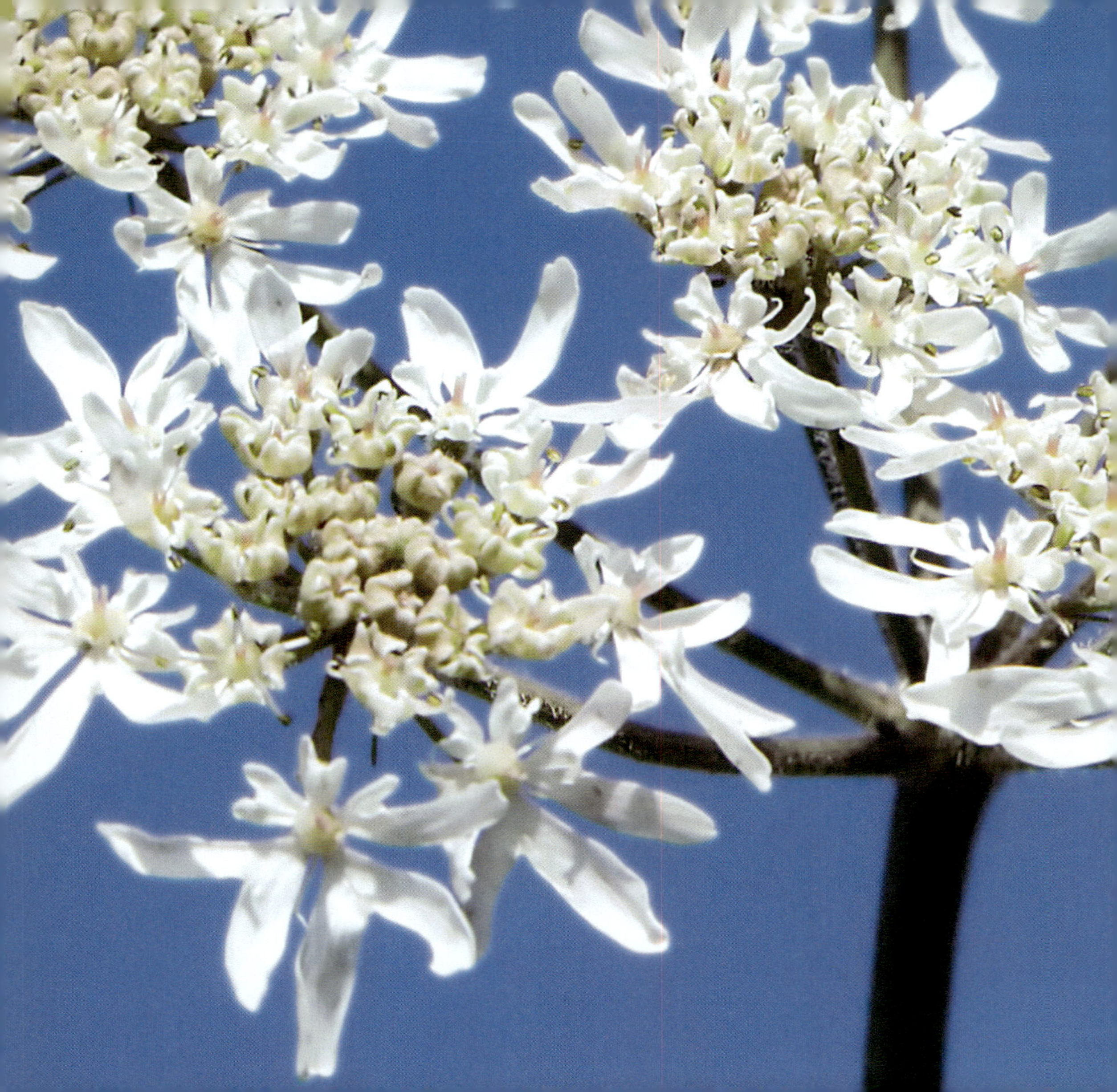

SWEET FLOWERS are slow
And weeds make haste

WILLIAM SHAKESPEARE, 1564-1616
RICHARD III

I HOPE TO LIVE TO SEE the day when I can expect to do my gardening, as tragedy is done, to slow and soothing music . . . I almost expect to find a cooling drink and hospitable entertainment at the end of a row. But I never do. There is nothing to be done but to hoe back to the other end.

CHARLES DUDLEY WARNER, 1829-1900

DON'T water your weeds

PROVERB

ONE OF THE PRETTIEST WEEDS that we have in our modern gardens, and which alternates between being our greatest joy and our greatest torment, is the Welsh Poppy. It succeeds so well in this dry soil that it sows itself everywhere; but when it stands up, with its profusion of yellow flowers well above its bed of bright green leaves, in some fortunate situation where it can not only be spared, but encouraged and admired, it is a real pleasure.

IN TALKING OF THE WELSH POPPY in July I spoke of it as one of the plants which are such weeds that at times one says, "Oh, I wish I had never introduced the horrible thing into my garden at all!" Another of these is the Campanula ranunculus, or Creeping Bell-flower — 'creeping' not because of its growth, but because of its root. After rain . . . I know nothing more lovely than the way it throws up its flower-stems, in quite unexpected places.

MRS C W EARLE, 1836-1925
POT-POURRI FROM A SURREY GARDEN

LIFE'S A GARDEN . . .
May all your weeds
be wild flowers

ANON

THE PEDIGREE of honey does not concern the bee;
A clover, any time, to him is aristocracy

EMILY DICKINSON, 1830-1886

IN THE GARDEN, THE USUAL FOREIGNERS gave place to the most scarce flowers, and especially to the rarer weeds, of Britain; and these were scattered here and there only for preservation . . . My father . . . passed much of his time among his choice weeds.

GEORGE CRABBE (THE YOUNGER), 1785-1857

I AM TOLD THAT abundant and rank weeds are signs of a rich soil, but I have noticed that a thin, poor soil grows little but weeds.

CHARLES DUDLEY WARNER, 1829-1900

FIE ON'T! O FIE! 'tis an unweeded garden
That grows to seed; things rank and gross in nature
Possess it merely.

WILLIAM SHAKESPEARE, 1564-1616
HAMLET

THE LITTLE YELLOW FUMITORY is invaluable for walls and dry places and under shrubs, always looking fresh and green and flourishing, however dry the weather or apparently unfavourable the situation. It is a weed, but it keeps away other weeds, which, as the old nurse said, was the great use of mothers — they kept away stepmothers.

MRS C W EARLE, 1836-1925
POT-POURRI FROM A SURREY GARDEN

A GARDEN is an awful responsibility. You never know what you might be aiding to grow in it

CHARLES DUDLEY WARNER, 1829-1900

LILY-OF-THE-VALLEY is the worst of all delicious weeds when it thrives

REGINALD FARRER, 1880-1920
THE ENGLISH ROCK GARDEN

HORSE-RADISH — as a weed, I know of nothing quite so pertinacious and pernicious as this: I know of nothing but fire which will destroy its powers of vegetation . . . But, as a vegetable, it is a very fine thing.

WILLIAM COBBETT, 1762-1835

LILIES THAT FESTER smell far worse than weeds

WILLIAM SHAKESPEARE, 1564-1616
SONNET 94

FOR GARDEN best
Is south south-west
Good tilth brings seedes
Evil Tilture weedes

THOMAS TUSSER, c. 1520-1580
FIVE HUNDRED POINTS OF GOOD HUSBANDRIE

AS IS THE GARDEN, such is the gardener
A man's nature runs either to herbs or weeds

FRANCIS BACON, 1561-1626

GENTLEWOMEN if the ground be not too wet, may doe themselves much good by Kneeling upon a Cushion and weeding. And thus both sexes might divert themselves from Idlenesse and evill company.

WILLIAM COLES, 1626-1662
THE ART OF SIMPLING

WEEDING, HOWING, ROLLING &c Above all, be carefull not to suffer weedes (especially Nettles, Dendelion, Groundsill, & all downy-plants) to run up to seede; for they will in a moment infect the whole ground: wherefore, whatever work you neglect, ply weeding at the first peeping of ye Spring. Malows, Thistles, Beane-bind, Couch must be grubb'd up and the ground forked & diligently pick'd. Whatever you How-up, rake-soone away off the ground, for most weedes will run to seede, and some rootes fasten again in the ground.

JOHN EVEYLN, 1620-1706

A GARDEN IS MAN'S ATTEMPT
to impose order on Nature.
Weeds are Nature's response.

GREG DUNCAN

ROSES ARE RED
Violets are blue
But they don't grow as fast
As those pesky weeds do

JENNY JONES

FLOWERS IN MY TIME which everyone would praise,
Though thrown like weeds from gardens now-a-days

JOHN CLARE, 1793-1864

THE MORNING PAST, we sweat beneath the sun;
And but uneasily our work goes on
Before us we perplexing thistles find . . .

STEPHEN DUCK, 1705-1756

THEN CAME OLD JANUARY, wrappèd well
In many weeds to keep the cold away

EDMUND SPENSER, 1552-1599
THE FAERIE QUEEN

MANY NEW GARDENERS, and even many of the more experienced gardeners, find it hard to distinguish between weed seedlings and valuable plants when they are weeding their borders. But there is a simple and well-known rule of thumb to help anyone tell the difference. Simply pull on the plant gently; if it comes out of the ground easily it is a valuable plant, if not, it is a weed.

ANOTHER TIME, too, with great labour, he cleared a considerable compartment of weeds, and when it looked clean and well, and he showed his work to the gardener, the man said he had demolished an asparagus bed! Mr d'A protested, however, nothing could look more like *les mauvais herbes*.

FANNY BURNEY, 1752-1840
LETTERS

THE STORY is told that when Gertrude Jekyll was young she had her own garden, and her mother taught her to distinguish the weed seedlings from the flower seedlings by cutting out paper patterns of the leaves of all the weeds, so that she would know which ones to pull up.

NO GARDEN is
without weeds

PROVERB

ON TAKING POSSESSION of our present abode, about four years ago, we found our garden, and all the gardens of the straggling village street in which it is situated, filled, peopled, infested by a beautiful flower, which grew in such profusion, and was so difficult to keep under, that (poor pretty thing!) instead of being admired and cherished and watered and supported, as it well deserves to be, and would be if it were rare, it is disregarded, affronted, maltreated, cut down, pulled up, hoed out, like a weed. I do not know the name of this elegant plant, nor have I met with any one who does; we call it the Spicer, after an old naval officer who once inhabited the white house just above, and, according to tradition, first brought the seed from foreign parts. It is a sort of large veronica, with a profusion of white gauzy flowers streaked with red, like the apple blossom. Strangers admire it prodigiously; and so do I — everywhere but in my own garden. I never saw anything prettier than a whole bed of these spicers, which had clothed the top of a large heap of earth belonging to our little mason by the road-side. Whether the wind had carried the light seed from his garden, or it had been thrown out in the mould, none could tell; but there grew the plants as thick and close as grass in a meadow, and covered with delicate red and white blossoms like a fairy orchard. I never passed without stopping to look at them; and, however accustomed to the work of extirpation in my own territories, I was one day half-shocked to see a man, his pockets stuffed with the plants, two huge bundles under each arm, and still tugging away root and branch. "Poor pretty flower," thought I, "not even suffered to enjoy the waste by the road-side! chased from the very common of nature, where the thistle and the nettle may spread and flourish! Poor despised flower!" This devastation did not, however, as I soon found, proceed from disrespect; the spicer-gatherer being engaged in sniffing with visible satisfaction to the leaves and stalks of the plant, which (although the blossom is wholly scentless) emit when bruised a very unpleasant odour. "It has a fine venomous smell," quothe he in soliloquy, "and will certainly when stilled be good for something or other."

MARY RUSSELL MITFORD, 1787-1865

A FLOWER without a name is a weed

KAREL CAPEK, 1890-1938

I AM MORE AND MORE IMPRESSED, as the summer goes on, with the inequality of man's fight with Nature . . . the minute he begins to clear a spot larger than he needs to sleep in for a night, and to try to have his own way in the least, Nature is at once up, and vigilant, and contests him at every step with all her ingenuity and unwearied vigour. This talk of subduing Nature is pretty much nonsense. I do not intend to surrender in the midst of the summer campaign, yet I cannot but think how much more peaceful my relations would now be with the primal forces if I had let Nature make the garden according to her own notion. (This is written with the thermometer at ninety degrees, and the weeds just starting up with a freshness and vigour, as if they had just thought of it for the first time, and had not been cut down and dragged out every other day since the snow went off.)

CHARLES DUDLEY WARNER, 1829-1900
MY SUMMER IN A GARDEN

EVERYONE has enough to do in weeding his own garden

FLEMISH PROVERB

OUR ENGLAND is a garden, and such gardens are not made
By singing: — "Oh, how beautiful!" and sitting in the shade,
While better men than we go out and start their working lives
At grubbing weeds from gravel-paths with broken dinner-knives.

There's not a pair of legs so thin, there's not a head so thick,
There's not a hand so weak and white, nor yet a heart so sick,
But it can find some needful job that's crying to be done,
For the Glory of the Garden glorifieth every one.

Oh, Adam was a gardener, and God who made him sees
That half a proper gardener's work is done upon his knees,
So when your work is finished, you can wash your hands and pray
For the Glory of the Garden, that it may not pass away!
And the Glory of the Garden, it shall never pass away!

RUDYARD KIPLING, 1865-1936
FROM: THE GLORY OF THE GARDEN

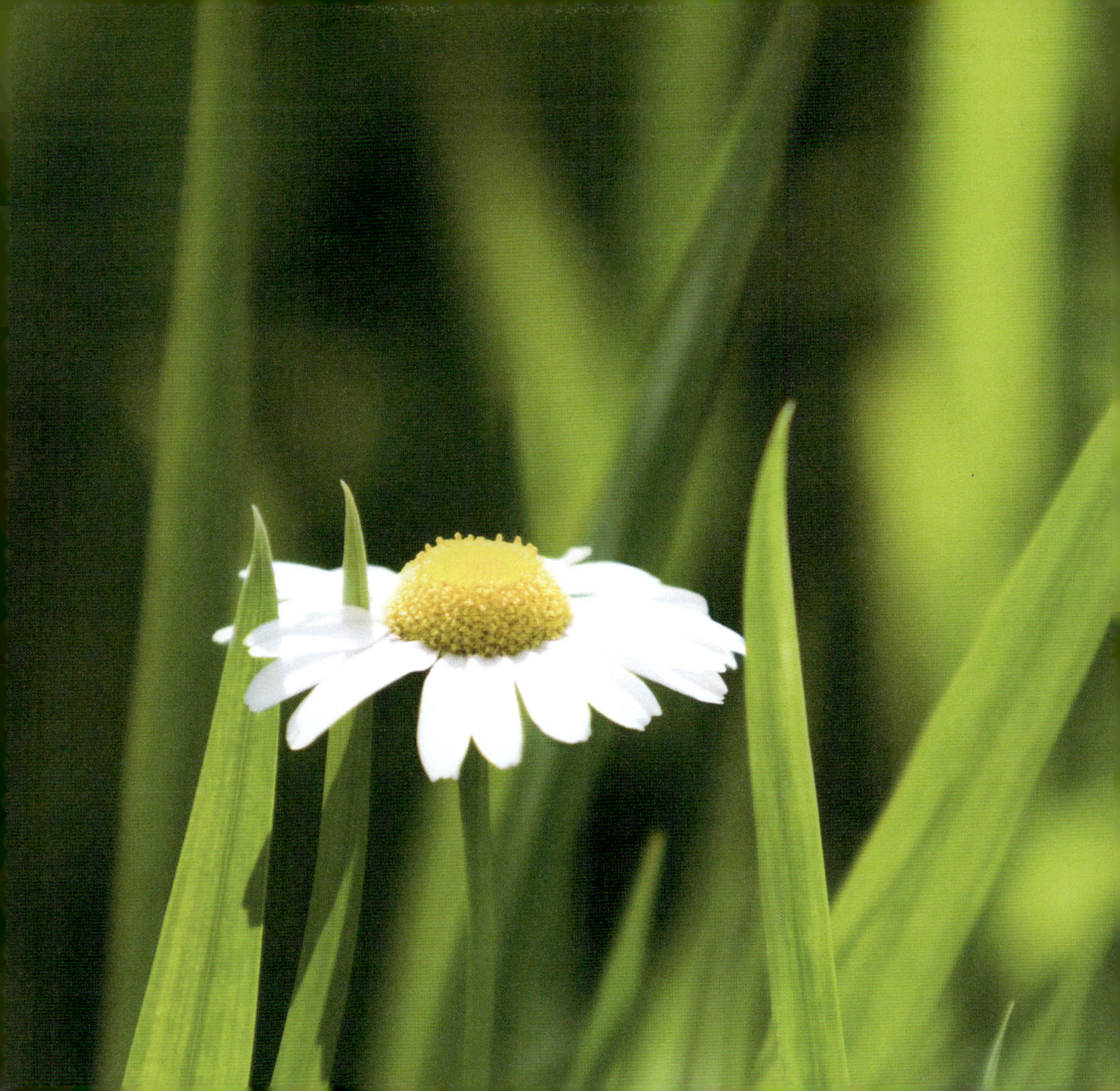

A MAN OF WORDS and not of deeds
Is like a garden full of weeds

PROVERB

SURELY God must love weeds,
for if he doesn't why would
he make so many of them?

JENNY JONES

LET YOUR PRAYERS for a good crop be short
. . . and your hoeing be long

PROVERB

WEEDING! What it means to us all! The worry of seeing the weeds, the labour of taking them up, the way they flourish at busy times, and the dangers that come from zeal without knowledge! When we first went to live in the country, an affectionate member of the family, who hates weeds and untidyness of all kinds, set to work to tear up ruthlessly every annual that had been sown, and with pride said, "At any rate, I have cleared that bit of ground."

MRS C W EARLE, 1836-1925
POT-POURRI FROM A SURREY GARDEN

SOME FOLKS think that weeding's a bore
It's a job they would rather ignore
But when weeding I find
My own peace of mind
And for me it is never a chore

LIMERICKS AND TRIMERICKS FOR GARDENERS

ONCE in a golden hour
I cast to earth a seed.
Up there came a flower,
The people said, a weed.

To and fro they went
Thro' my garden-bower
And muttering discontent
Cursed me and my flower.

Then it grew so tall
It wore a crown of light,
But thieves from o'er the wall
Stole the seed by night.

Sow'd it far and wide
By every town and tower
Till all the people cried,
"Splendid is the flower."

Read my little fable:
He that runs may read.
Most can raise the flowers now,
For all have got the seed.

And some are pretty enough,
And some are poor indeed;
And now again the people
Call it but a weed.

ALFRED, LORD TENNYSON, 1809-1892
THE FLOWER

WEEDS ARE people's idea, not nature's

ANON

FREE WEEDS
pick your own

THE WEEDS . . . have hateful moral qualities. To cut down a weed is, therefore, to do a moral action. I feel as if I were destroying sin. My hoe becomes an instrument of retributive justice. I am an apostle of Nature. This view of the matter lends a dignity to the art of hoeing which nothing else does, and lifts it into the region of ethics. Hoeing becomes not a pastime, but a duty. And you get to regard it so, as the days and the weeds lengthen.

CHARLES DUDLEY WARNER, 1829-1900
MY SUMMER IN A GARDEN

EVERYONE comes to a garden party
Enthusiasts come to a planting party
But no one comes to a weeding party

WHY is it slugs prefer flowers to weeds?

OH HOW I'VE TUGGED and pulled at the twisted roots of nettles in my wild garden, following the stringy yellow fibres a yard or more along the ground; or worse still have been my struggles with 'ground elder', which made its way everywhere. It was a yearly toil, but at last I conquered, and made the weeds understand that although wild, yet it was a flower and not a 'bear garden'.

THE HON MRS EVELYN CECIL, 1865-1941
CHILDREN'S GARDENS

MY GARDEN'S an interesting place
To watch the inevitable race
Between all the flowers
I've tended for hours
And the weeds which are growing apace

LIMERICKS AND TRIMERICKS FOR GARDENERS

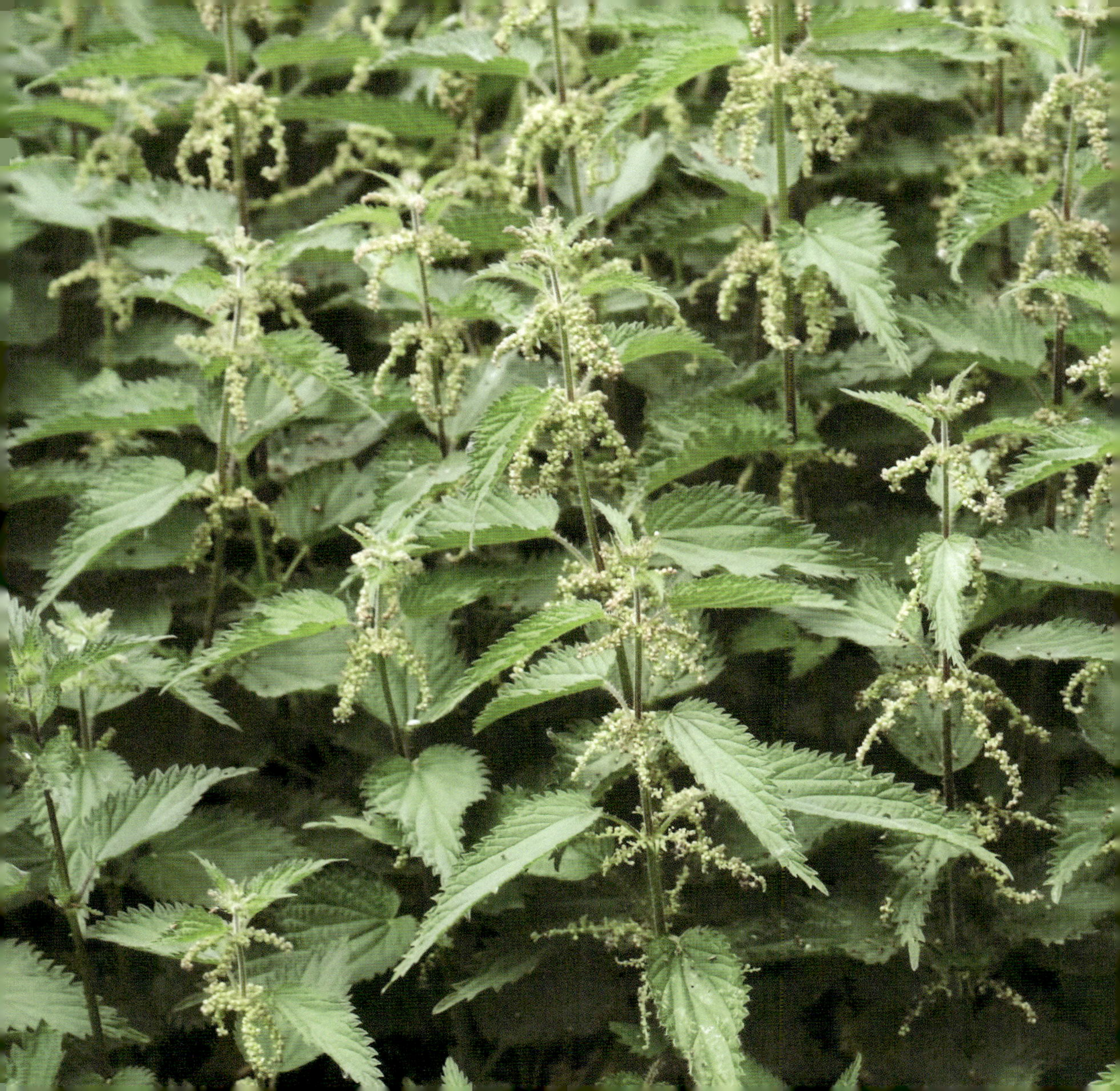

SO MANY weeds
So little time

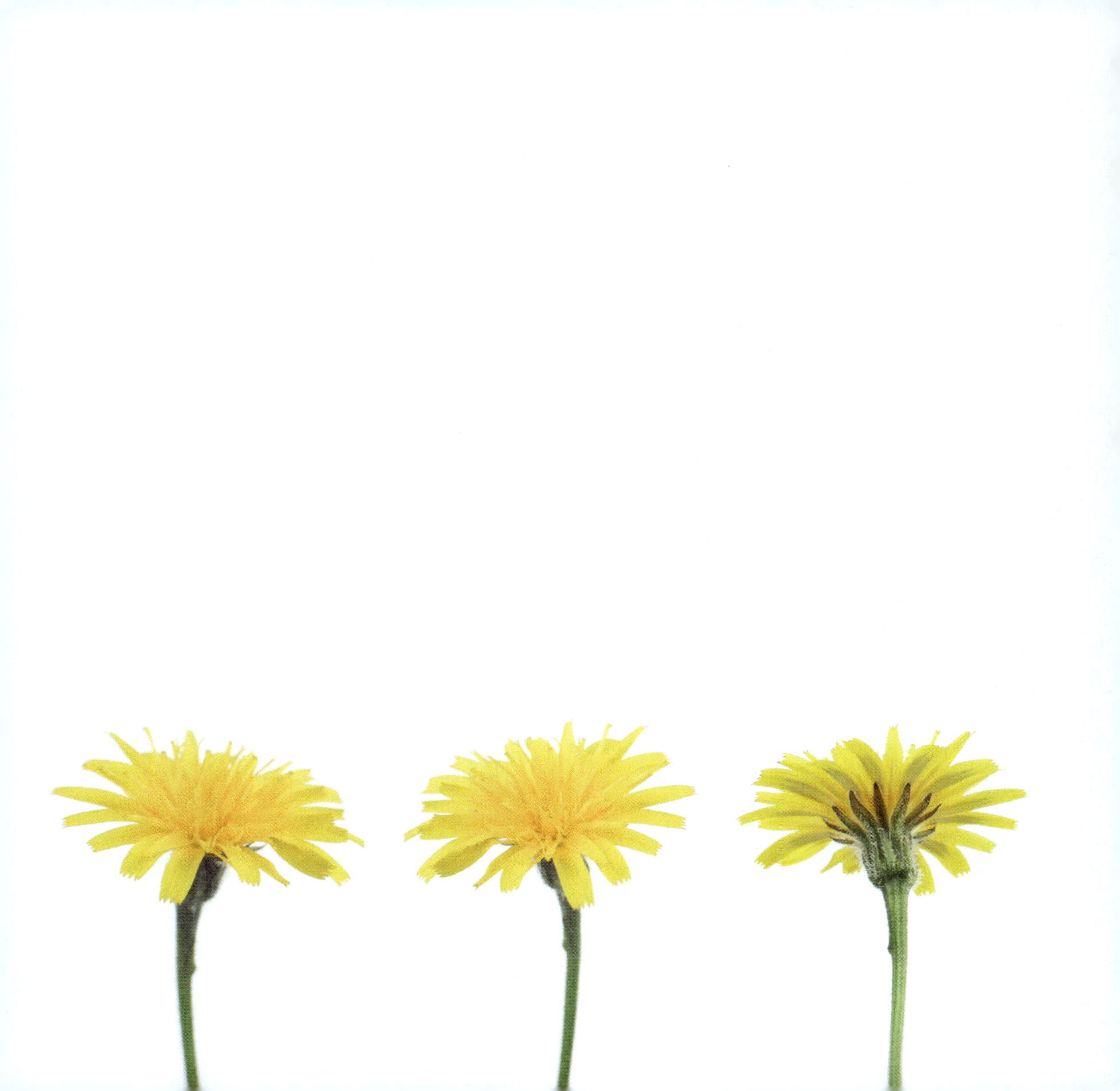

This edition published by Kenebec Media 2020

www.kenebec.com/books

This compilation © Val and Greg Duncan 2020
Photographs © Val and Greg Duncan 2020
Text by Val Duncan and Greg Duncan © Val and Greg Duncan 2020

The moral rights of the authors have been asserted. All rights reserved. No parts of this publication may be reproduced, stored in a retrieval system or transmitted, in any form or by any means, electronic, mechanical, photocopying, recording or otherwise, without the prior written permission of the publishers.

ISBN: 9798649584852

The 'K' symbol is a registered trade mark of Kenebec Ltd.

X105

Printed in Poland
by Amazon Fulfillment
Poland Sp. z o.o., Wrocław